Blogger's Quick Guide to Blog Post Ideas

SET UP SYSTEMS, NURTURE CREATIVITY, AND NEVER RUN OUT OF BLOG POST IDEAS AGAIN

Rebecca Livermore

Professional Content Creation

ISBN-13: 978-1545457818

ISBN-10: 1545457816

Blogger's Quick Guide to Blog Post Ideas

Copyright © 2017 by Rebecca Livermore

All rights reserved. No part of this publication may be reproduced, stored in a retrieval system, or transmitted by any means – electronic, mechanical, photographic (photocopying), recording, or otherwise – without prior permission in writing from the author.

Learn more information at:

http://professionalcontentcreation.com

Table of Contents

Blogger's Quick Guide to Blog Post Ideas 1

Table of Contents 3

Introduction 1

SET UP A BLOG POST IDEA CAPTURE SYSTEM 5

Analog or Digital 7

Analog Tools 9

Digital Tools 13

NURTURE CREATIVITY 23

Sleep 25

Artist Dates 27

Mindless Activity 29

Freewrite 31

Do Something Creative, Just for Fun 33

Enjoy Nature 35

Exercise and Eat Properly 37

Feed Your Spirit 39

Take Public Transportation 41

Be a Life-Long Learner 43

Develop Your Own Blogging Rituals 45

HOW TO COME UP WITH IDEAS 47

Brainstorm 49

Templates 51

Speeches, Sermons, and YouTube Videos 53

Reading Notes 55

Reviews 57

Movie Reviews and Character Studies 59

Case Studies 61

Your Successes and Failures 63

Stories 65

Spin-Off Posts 67

Holidays and Special Events 69

They Ask, You Answer 71

Use Any Object 73

Blog a Book 77

Other People's Content 79

Curate Your Own Content 83

Update and Repurpose Old Content 85

Interviews 87

Get Guest Contributors 89

Series Articles 93

Trends 95

Weekly or Monthly Themes 97

Ultimate List Posts 99

Divide Posts 101

Use the Researcher Option in Microsoft Word 103

Comments on Blog Posts, YouTube Videos, and Facebook Groups 105

Experiences of Friends and Family 107

Amazon 109

Blog Post Title Generators 111

Jargon 113

Keyword Tools 115

Be Negative 117

Evaluating and Using Ideas 119

Conclusion 121

Introduction

WHEN IT COMES TO RUNNING A SUCCESSFUL BLOG, coming up with blog post ideas is half the battle. In my experience with blogging I've found that as long as I have an idea for what to write about, it's pretty easy for me to sit down and do it. However, when I have no clue what to write about, the empty page and the blinking cursor seem to mock me. That's when the dreaded writer's block strikes.

The good news is, it's possible to have an endless – yes, endless – supply of blog post ideas. The key is to have ways to generate ideas and a system in place for capturing and organizing ideas. And that is what this book is all about.

Why Your Ideas Matter

Before I get into the structure of this book, I want to address a major issue: your ideas matter.

Maybe it's just me, but if I'm totally honest, in my heart of hearts, sometimes I fear that I have nothing unique to offer to the world. I share that with you because if you ever feel that way, I want you to know you're not alone.

I also want to share the truth with you that I've discovered, and that is that my ideas matter – and so do yours. We are each unique. No one else on the planet can offer what we can. Sure, there may be other bloggers – perhaps even very successful ones – that blog on the same topic we do. But no one – and I mean NO ONE – has your unique gifts and personality. No one else sees the world exactly the same way you do. No one has your insight. Your gift, your insight, your "you-ness" is a gift the world needs. And your blog is one of the best ways to share that gift with the world.

People Are Looking for Solutions You Offer

I also want you to understand and embrace the fact that people are looking for the solutions that you offer. Regardless of your niche, your passion, your business or ministry, people need your knowledge and insight.

Be encouraged by how much you matter and how important it is to unleash the ideas that are buried deep inside you. My goal is for you to unearth and shine up those ideas as a result of reading this book.

How This Book Is Structured

I divided this book into the following three parts:

#1: How to Set up a Blog Post Idea Capture System
- Analog Tools
- Digital Tools

In this section, I get into the pros and cons of analog and digital tools for capturing blog post ideas. I also share some of my favorite tools with you.

#2: How to Nurture Creativity

Stress and the regular day-to-day grind can run our creativity well dry. In this section, I get into ways to recharge and refuel, and how to live life in such a way that creativity flows.

#3: How to Come Up with Ideas

This section is the meat of the book. I include over 30 methods for generating blog post ideas. Regardless of your personality and your work style, in this section, you're sure to find ways to generate blog post ideas that are perfect for you.

The book concludes with suggestions for evaluating and using the blog post ideas that you generate.

Developing the Blogging Habit

By the way, as I mentioned above, coming up with blog post ideas is half the battle. The other half of the battle is making blogging a habit. As a companion to this book, I've created the free e-course, 5 Secrets to Developing the Blogging Habit, which you can get here:

http://www.professionalcontentcreation.com/blogging-habit/

Without further ado, let's go ahead and dive in!

Blogger's Quick Guide to Blog Post Ideas. . • 4

SET UP A BLOG POST IDEA CAPTURE SYSTEM

Before I get into how to come up with blog post ideas, I want to first give you some options for setting up a way to capture all of your ideas. I'm putting this first because you can come up with a gazillion ideas, but if you don't have a good way to capture them, you won't be able to find them when you need them.

Blogger's Quick Guide to Blog Post Ideas. . • 6

Analog or Digital

When choosing the tools, you want to use, one thing to consider is whether you want to use an analog or digital system. Some people swear by the value of doing it the old-fashioned way and writing everything out by hand.

I personally prefer to do everything digitally. If you are a Microsoft Windows user and have a 2-in-1 PC, you have the best of both worlds. That's what I do myself. I have a Microsoft Surface Book, so I can type in it, or I can use it as a tablet and handwrite.

While I prefer digital, to be honest with you, there are some significant advantages to old-fashioned analog. For instance, today as I was working on this book, my electricity went out, and at the same time, so did my Internet. Suddenly, I felt stuck. I had a tough time working because my entire process is digital.

Another example of a digital fail is, earlier this week, the battery in the pen that I use with my computer died, so I've been unable to handwrite anything on my computer while waiting for a new battery to show up in the mail.

These two recent events serve as a reminder to me that while I love all the digital tools we have available, there are times when nothing beats old-fashioned pen and paper.

Do What Works Best for You

As is always the case, the main thing is to do whatever works best for you. If, like me, you prefer digital, don't lay a guilt trip on yourself every time you read or hear that analog is better. On the other hand, if you actually do prefer old-fashioned paper and pen, don't feel like you're out of it or wrong for being old-school.

The primary thing is to find a tool or at the most (as I'll explain a bit later) two tools that work well for you.

Having said that, here are some tools you might want to try.

Analog Tools

IF YOU WANT TO GO THE ANALOG ROUTE, here are some analog tools from which to choose.

Paper and Pen

Let's start off with the most basic tools: paper and pen or pencil. These are the tools I recommend the least. Why? Because it's easy to lose track of your ideas if you write them on **random** pieces of paper.

For example, let's say that sometimes you grab a piece of notebook paper and jot down an idea. The next time you're near your printer, you grab a piece of printer paper and make a note of your great idea. On another day, you're out to lunch with a friend or enjoying coffee alone at a coffee shop and you jot an idea on a napkin.

Unless you're a lot more organized than I am, those pieces of paper will end up scattered hither and yon, and they'll end up in the trash or stuffed in a drawer somewhere, never to be looked at again.

Journal, Notebook, or Notepad

If you like to write on paper, instead of using random pieces of paper as described above, consider investing in a journal or a notebook. If you decide to go the notebook route, consider using a notebook that is small enough to fit in your purse, pocket or computer case. The idea is that you want to take your "idea collection bucket" with you everywhere you go because you never know when an idea will strike!

If you decide to use a journal or notebook, consider creating a table of contents or index in the front or back pages.

3x5 Cards

3x5 cards are a popular choice for those who go the analog route. The wonderful thing about them is that they are small enough to fit into a pocket or anything else you like to carry, such as a purse. They are also sturdier than most paper and are also a uniform size and shape, which makes them less likely to end up lost or accidentally tossed.

Another great thing about 3x5 cards is that you can use one side for the main idea and the other side to jot down notes about the idea. For example, on the back of the card, you may jot down general thoughts about the idea, where to get more information, someone to call to interview, etc.

Ways to Organize Your 3x5 Cards

Binder Ring: If you decide to go the 3x5 card route, consider buying a hole punch and a binder ring. The binder ring will hold all your cards together and allow you to flip through them easily.

Recipe Box: A file box is another great way to store your 3x5 cards. Depending on the size of the file box, you can store up to several hundred cards in each box. File boxes often come with dividers, which will help you organize your cards. For example, you can put tabs in your recipe box for different months of the year or for blog post categories.

Photo Album: Old-fashioned photo albums have sleeves where you can insert photos – or 3x5 cards. Photo albums are assorted sizes so you could potentially even have one small enough to fit into a purse or backpack if you want. However, I personally think they are too bulky to carry around, so I would most likely leave my photo album in my home or office.

Binder Clip: In a pinch, you can just use a binder clip or a rubber band to hold your cards together. The reason why I mention this as a last resort is that you must remove the binder clip/rubber band to look through your cards. While that's not a big deal, what often happens, in this case, is that the binder clip or rubber band gets lost or you forget to put it back on, and your cards may end up scattered.

If think that you want to try the 3x5 card method and happen to have some cards and a rubber band or binder clip in your home or office, go for it! Sometimes striking while the iron's hot and getting started right away is more important than having the perfect tools. Plan to upgrade to one of the other options as soon as possible.

Whiteboard

I know people who have entire walls that are whiteboards! If you don't want to go to that extreme, there are whiteboards available in many different sizes.

One whiteboard option you may want to consider is one with a calendar on it. For example, I have a large whiteboard with a calendar that has a corkboard that runs along the bottom of the whiteboard. To the left of the calendar is a blank area, where I can add random notes. Except for the cork part, the entire board is magnetic, which provides yet another way to store paper notes.

Sticky Notes

A lot of people love sticky notes. And there's a lot to love about them. For example, nowadays you can buy them in multiple shapes, sizes, and colors. And, naturally, as the name implies, you can stick them on things!

The wonderful thing about sticky notes is that you can use them in conjunction with a whiteboard or poster board. This enables you to rearrange them in many ways. For example, perhaps you'll start off with a full board of random blog post ideas on sticky notes, and then later go in and arrange them by month or theme or in some other way.

Paper Mind Map

Paper mind maps are great for doing brain dumps. You can create a mind map on a regular size piece of paper, such as a page in a notebook or a piece of printer paper. If you want to mind map several ideas, you can buy a large roll of paper and tape it to the wall.

Again, this method is best for brainstorming sessions, rather than regular idea capturing.

Digital Tools

IF GOING ANALOG ISN'T FOR YOU, in this chapter, I'll get into some of the top digital tools for capturing blog post ideas.

WordPress Plugins

If you use WordPress as your blogging platform of choice, you may want to consider **CoSchedule.** CoSchedule is not a free plugin, but it has a lot of great features when it comes to managing your blog and social media content.

You can "dump" a bunch of ideas in it that you can then schedule for a specific date or leave it without a date. If you leave it without a date, you can scan through all of the post ideas without an assigned date when you need an idea for a blog post.

You can also use this free editorial calendar plugin: https://wordpress.org/plugins/editorial-calendar/. While this plugin doesn't have all the bells and whistles of CoSchedule, it's a great, lightweight editorial calendar plugin, and since it's a free tool, the price is certainly right.

Evernote

Evernote is one of the most popular note taking, idea capturing, programs out there. You can get it free at https://evernote.com/.

There are several ways to use Evernote. For example, you can use it to send blog posts from the web. If you're reading a blog post and you think, "This has some great information for me to reference in my blog," send it to Evernote! If you like to freewrite and want to keep track of your freewriting, you can do it in Evernote! There are many, many ways to use Evernote for capturing ideas. A big plus of Evernote is that it's such a popular app and it integrates with a lot of other programs.

OneNote

OneNote is what I like to refer to as the Microsoft version of Evernote. I personally switched to OneNote from Evernote because it works in a way that fits better with my personal learning and organizational style.

OneNote has many of the same features as Evernote, such as being able to clip blog posts and send them to OneNote, the ability to freewrite or compose entire blog posts, and so on.

In addition to that, it has a "dock to desktop" option that makes note taking while watching a webinar or video or while reading blog posts a breeze. When you use the dock-to-desktop option, your OneNote note is in the right part of your monitor, and you can watch videos, read blog posts, etc. that are on the left side of your monitor. If you've ever had the experience of trying to take notes in Word, Notepad, or some other program only to have your document disappear when you click "play" on the video, you'll appreciate the dock-to-desktop option in OneNote.

Another favorite feature is that if you have a device with a touch screen, such as a Windows 2-in-1 PC, you can also handwrite and draw in OneNote.

Finally, I find it easier to organize content in OneNote because you can rearrange pages by dragging them into whatever order you want rather than the alphabetical or number organization system used in Evernote.

The bottom line is both OneNote and Evernote are great options for keeping track of everything in your life, including blog post ideas. Since they are similar in many regards, unless you're already invested in one of them, I recommend experimenting with each of them to determine which one suits your preference.

Note that both Evernote and OneNote are available for both Mac and PC as well as Android, iOS, and Windows phones and tablets.

You can download OneNote for free at https://www.onenote.com/download.

Wunderlist

Wunderlist is another popular option for tracking blog post ideas. I haven't personally used it, but my friend Marylee Pangman uses it and loves it. I asked her to share how she uses it for capturing blog post ideas, and here is what she wrote:

I have used many different methods for task organization. Blogging success definitely relies on keeping one foot in front of the other to stay on task. After rejecting several different apps and systems, I revisited Wunderlist. Earlier, I thought it pretty weak in its organization of my tasks. What I was looking for and still rely on are the following criteria:

- Ability to have categories and sub-categories.

- Syncs with my Google calendar on a constant sync basis. Some apps only sync once in 24 hours (this is something to watch for).

- Easy to navigate and reorganize.

- Operates easily and syncs readily with apps between my PC, iPad and iPhone.

- Free is always nice.

Wunderlist does all of these things. There is one point I don't prefer but I will get to that later. You can set up the organization of Wunderlist to your personal preferences, follow GTD (Getting Things Done) methods or even Kanban.

For blogging, I have two domains that I blog on. I set up a Wunderlist folder for each of these domain blogs. Within each folder, I created individual lists for the following categories:

- My Blog Ideas
- Blog Ideas from Other Sources
- Draft Blog (the one I am currently working on)
- Blogs Ready to be Published (with title and location)
- Blogs Published (with title and location)

It is easy to move a task that originated in "My Blog Ideas" and turn it into a "Draft Blog" task and subsequently "Ready to be Published" and "Published."

You can set a due date as well as a recurring task date, which is great to set writing tasks for as many days a week as you want. You can also set a reminder to alert you to do a task at a specific time.

Wunderlist also has a place for notes, each task can be divided into subtasks and you can add links, pictures or anything else you want within the task.

The only drawback to Wunderlist is that when it syncs to my calendar, it goes up at the top into the all-day events area. I'd rather have it down during the time period I plan on working on that task. Reminders help but it does not show your day accurately.

That being said, Wunderlist meets all of my preferred criteria. There is a paid version, but unless you have a complex organization with a large team, I don't see the need to spend the money. If you are looking for a good way to organize your task and blogging world, give Wunderlist a try!

Marylee Pangman
Business Advisor, Coach, and Author
Blossomosity.com

Scrivener

Scrivener is a popular program for writing books, but some top bloggers, such as Michael Hyatt, have used it for blogging as well.

To be honest, while many bloggers and authors swear by Scrivener, and I'm sure it's a great program, it's complex enough that I never really got the hang of it.

However, since it's so popular and so many people love it, I wanted to include it here as a tool to consider.

If you do decide to use Scrivener, there are a couple of ways you can go about it. For instance, instead of starting a project for a book, you can start one project that is for a particular blog post category, one to keep links to different articles and so on.

FreeMind

FreeMind is the mindmapping tool that I use. I don't personally use it for collecting blog post ideas. However, I do use it for brain dumps and to plan books.

If you haven't mindmapped before, it's worth trying. The essential way that it works is to put a central idea in the middle of the "page," and then link out to related content from there. For example, if I were to use FreeMind for my blog, I might just put the name of my blog in the center, and then link out to various categories from there.

The best thing about mind maps is that it's very easy to rearrange the ideas, simply by dragging and dropping. So, you can do an initial brain dump of ideas in no particular order and then organize them, for example, by blog post category.

A significant limitation of mind maps is that you can't write much for each idea. For instance, if an idea that I had for a blog post had to do with optimizing a blog post for SEO, the words "How to Optimize a Blog Post for SEO" would be all that I would put on the mind map. If I had additional ideas about what to include in the post, I could handle it in one of two ways:

- Create another node for each idea
- Link a node to a document where I flesh out the idea.

Due to this limitation, it's not my favorite for anything more than brain dumps where the only goal is to jot down as many ideas as possible in a short period of time.

But as the name implies FreeMind is indeed free, so it won't hurt to give it a shot. You can download FreeMind here: https://sourceforge.net/projects/freemind/

PowerPoint

I'm a big fan of Microsoft Office for content creation, and PowerPoint is no exception.

As I explain in this article and video:

http://www.professionalcontentcreation.com/powerpoint-as-an-editorial-calendar/ you can use PowerPoint as an editorial calendar and in a similar way use it to organize your blog post ideas. For blog post ideas, I recommend using a section for each of the categories for your blog and then adding a slide under the appropriate category section for each blog post idea.

Pinterest

Pinterest is a great place to gather ideas that inspire you. A huge limitation is that you need to link to blog posts and other online content, and there isn't a lot of room to write your ideas. But in terms of a way to "bookmark" and organize content that inspires you and that you may want to use as a jumping off point in your content brainstorming and creation, it's a great option.

By the way, you can create private Pinterest boards if you don't want your collections to be made public.

OneDrive and Google Drive

I put these two options together because they are similar in a lot of ways.

Essentially, they can both be used to create and store Word, Excel and PowerPoint documents. The Google Drive version uses their own "knock-off" versions of these programs. OneDrive also includes OneNote notebooks as an option, so if you like organizing things with notebooks, OneNote is a better option for you.

Both have free and premium options available, with the primary difference between free and premium being the amount of storage.

Both Google Drive and OneDrive allow you to share your documents with other users so if you collaborate on your content with other team members and want to share documents with them, you can easily do so. For example, let's say you come up with the blog post ideas and another team member creates featured images for the content and another does some research for you; everyone on your team can have access to the documents.

If you happen to have an Office365 account, you may have as much as 1TB of storage in OneDrive for free, depending on the type of Office365 account that you have. Even if you're super prolific and come up with a ridiculous amount of blog post ideas, the free version has plenty of storage. However, if you want to store a lot of other things, such as photos and videos in the same place, OneDrive is an excellent option. For that reason, and because OneDrive uses official Microsoft Office documents, I switched from Google Drive to OneDrive.

You can get them here:

https://www.google.com/drive/

https://onedrive.live.com

Spreadsheets

Spreadsheets have been used to organize information since the beginning of time. Well, that's a bit of an exaggeration, since spreadsheets have only been around since the late 1970s. But bloggers have used spreadsheets for a very long time as editorial calendars, and they can certainly be used to store your blog post ideas.

If you're going to use spreadsheets, I recommend using spreadsheets in either Google Drive or OneDrive rather than a local copy on your computer so that you can access them from anywhere.

Tags

By the way, if you decide to go the digital route, use tags whenever possible to help you find things later. For example, in both OneNote and Evernote, you can tag notes and later search for that specific tag. As an example, since I write on Microsoft Office for creatives, I might use a tag such as "OneNote" if I have a blog post idea related to OneNote.

Use One (or at the most two) System(s)

When it comes to setting up a system for tracking ideas, ultimately you want to have one place where all your ideas reside. For example, you'll want to put all your ideas in a paper notebook or put all your ideas in a digital notebook, such as Evernote, or my favorite, OneNote.

The alternative to this is that you can have one method for quickly jotting down your ideas, and then another tool where you keep all your ideas.

For example, let's say you like to write your ideas on 3x5 cards, and you always have some in your pocket or purse or on your nightstand. But let's say that you also like to use an online notebook such as OneNote where you save things like blog posts that you'll use as inspiration or for reference. In this case, I recommend you use OneNote as your primary location. Ultimately, you'll put all your ideas into OneNote. Then, have scheduled times, such as daily, weekly, or monthly, where you add the ideas from your notecards into OneNote.

The reason this is important is that you want to reduce the time you spend trying to find where you put your ideas. If you have ideas written on the backs of napkins, in a notebook, in Word documents, on 3x5 cards, and in OneNote, when it comes time to find your ideas, or to locate a specific idea, you'll waste a lot of time searching for your ideas in the various places you have them.

Is There an App for That?

Ideally, if you go the digital route, your primary system for storing your ideas should be accessible on all your devices and on any computer with an Internet connection.

The key thing to look for in this regard is:

- Web app for the program

- Phone and tablet apps for the same program

As an example, I can access all my documents that I've stored on OneDrive from any computer with an Internet connection, and I can also access those same documents from my phone since there is a OneDrive app for my phone.

Of the different tools mentioned earlier in this chapter, here are the ones that meet that criterion:

- Google Drive

- OneDrive
- Evernote
- OneNote
- Trello
- Scrivener
- Wunderlist
- FreeMind (There isn't an official FreeMind app, but there are Android apps that claim to be compatible)

Assignment

Select two ways of capturing ideas. Make sure one way is something you can use all the time, including when you're out and about.

The second way needs to be where you put all the ideas you've collected, including the ones you get when you're away from your home or office.

NURTURE CREATIVITY

Have you ever sat down to write but felt almost dead inside? Let's face it, you probably wouldn't be reading this book, and I most certainly wouldn't have chosen to write it, if it wasn't for the fact that a lot of bloggers struggle with coming up with ideas.

Part of the problem with coming up with blog post ideas is that our well is dry. It's hard to draw water from a well if the well is filled with nothing but stones and dry, cracked soil. Because of that, it's important to intentionally nurture your blogging soul.

Sleep

SLEEP, OR THE LACK THEREOF, has an enormous impact on creativity. If you don't sleep well, you can't expect to think and come up with ideas.

Unfortunately, many of us cut corners when it comes to sleep. This is especially true if you have young children. In fact, if you have a newborn, you're almost guaranteed to be sleep deprived.

For the rest of us, lack of sleep is often a symptom of a lack of discipline. I know for myself, when I end up staying up way too late, the cause is often as trivial as having gone down a YouTube rabbit hole. I start watching videos and keep saying, "Just one more," until before you know it, it's two hours past my regular bedtime.

Now, of course, there are times when getting to bed late can't be helped. For instance, maybe you're out at an event that ends late, and it takes time to get home and unwind. Or you may have some pressing work or a client deadline that requires staying up late. But most of the time, if you have the discipline, you can get to bed on time.

Something that has helped me in this regard is to set an alarm on my phone to go off an hour before lights-out time. At that time, I start my "before bed routine." My before bed routine includes washing and moisturizing my face, drinking a nice hot cup of magnesium (I use Natural Calm in hot water) or chamomile tea, getting my jammies on, and sitting in bed reading. I also sometimes do a bit of doodling or other simple artwork that is "just for me." The just-for-me aspect is important because then I can focus on relaxing and enjoying the process, rather than worrying about creating something beautiful. It is also helpful to shut down electronic devices such as your phone and computer an hour before bed.

Your bedtime routine may look very different than mine, but it should be relaxing and help you transition from wakefulness to sleep.

Artist Dates

I FIRST LEARNED ABOUT THE CONCEPT of artist dates in the book *The Artist's Way* by Julia Cameron. An artist date is simply a time where you are intentional about refueling. Cameron recommends doing it alone.

I first started going on artist dates when my now-grown children were young. I was a stay-at-home mom, and these times alone were vital not just for my creativity but also for my sanity! At that time, most often my weekly artist date was merely going to a coffee shop with my journal. I sipped coffee, daydreamed, and journaled. Occasionally, I brought a book to read as well.

Here are some other artist date ideas:

- Visit a local nursery and browse. Some nurseries have fountains that add to the ambiance and relaxing environment.

- Take a walk on the beach and gather sea shells.

- Go to an art museum.

- If you live in an older city, take a walk downtown or in older neighborhoods and pay attention to details that you often fail to see such as interesting architecture on seemingly mundane things like doors.

- Visit a botanical garden. Take a sketchbook and pens or pencils and sketch some of the flowers and other plants – even if you feel like you can't draw!

- Go to a concert or play.

- Sit in a park or café, and people watch.

- Go for a massage, pedicure or manicure.

- Handwrite a letter to someone who means a lot to you and mail it to them.

- Go fly a kite.

- Visit an ethnic grocery store and pick up some ingredients to make something you've never eaten before. You may want to find a recipe first, so you know what to buy.

- Lay in a hammock or on a blanket underneath a shade tree and read.

- Visit an art supply store and browse around. Pick up some new supplies. It doesn't have to be anything fancy or expensive. Even a new pen in a color you like works.

- Go out for ice cream and try a new flavor that "sounds weird." For example, a small, independently-owned ice cream shop near me has flavors like strawberry basil. Sounds weird, but it tastes delicious!

You get the idea! The main thing is to do something you don't normally do, or only do on your artist dates. It should be fun and relaxing, and something you do alone. While you can do many of these activities with a friend, spouse, or other family member, being alone gives you the space to daydream and think about things rather than feeling like you need to pay attention to someone else. It also gives you the freedom to spend as much or as little time as you want, or to switch gears and do something different than you originally planned.

You can do an artist date whenever you want, but as typically happens in life, if you don't plan for it, it doesn't get done.

Mindless Activity

NOWADAYS, OUR MINDS ARE BOMBARDED with an unending amount of stimuli. Everything from social media to email to billboards, music and more; it seems to never stop.

One of the best ways to nurture creativity is to simply turn all of that off. The good news is, you can do so while also going about your business doing things you need to do anyway. For example, taking a shower is a regular, recurring and necessary event, but it's a great time to nurture creativity.

Here are a few other "mindless" things you can and likely should do on a regular basis.

- Running or walking
- Dishes
- Other housework
- Gardening
- Decluttering

The key with all these is to have something to write on nearby when doing these activities so you can quickly jot them down. For example, you can buy waterproof whiteboards and notepads to use in the shower. You can also have whiteboards in various rooms of the house, such as your kitchen, and carry a small notebook or phone to record ideas when you're out and about.

Freewrite

PEOPLE OFTEN REFER TO FREEWRITING as stream of consciousness writing. When you freewrite, you write without judgment, and you write nonstop for a particular period of time, such as 15 minutes. There aren't a whole lot of rules when it comes to freewriting. The only real rule is to write nonstop. If you can't think of something to say, just write things like "I can't think of what to write. This is stupid. I don't like this" or any other random thing that pops into your head.

I give more freewriting tips in my free e-course *5 Secrets to Developing the Blogging Habit*, which you can check out here: http://www.professionalcontentcreation.com/blogging-habit/

One of the best things about freewriting is that since it's not focused on quality or accomplishing something specific, it makes it much easier to write every day, and writing in and of itself increases creativity.

Do Something Creative, Just for Fun

DO SOMETHING CREATIVE, that's unrelated to how you make a living. For example, I know very little about photography and would likely never make money through photography, so heading out with my camera can feed my blogging soul. Since I don't know enough about photography to look critically at any photos I take, I can enjoy myself when I pick up my camera.

I've also started taking some drawing classes on Skillshare, and I can't draw a straight line to save my life! But as much as possible, I spend some time drawing every day. This not only relieves stress, but it helps my overall creativity, and that spills over into my writing life as well.

By the way, at the current time, you can access thousands of classes on Skillshare that will nurture your creativity, for just 99 cents for the first month. Here's a link to my courses: https://www.skillshare.com/r/user/rlivermore, but since you have access to ALL courses for the same price, don't limit yourself to what I offer. While you're there, be sure to check out courses on doodling, photography, or anything else your creative heart desires!

Blogger's Quick Guide to Blog Post Ideas. . • 34

Enjoy Nature

I'M A CITY GIRL AND KNOW VERY LITTLE about nature, but getting outside and taking a walk in a beautiful place can feed my blogging soul. I live a block away from a beautiful park, and every time I go there, I end up inspired and refreshed.

Other nearby options for me include botanical gardens, and even garden shops if weather is not conducive to outdoor activities. You can do this as part of the artist dates mentioned above, but it doesn't have to be big.

Even a short stroll in the park or going outside and looking at the trees, the sky, etc. for five minutes works!

Blogger's Quick Guide to Blog Post Ideas. . • 36

Exercise and Eat Properly

I PUT PROPER EATING AND EXERCISE TOGETHER because, for me, those two tend to go together. If I'm watching what I eat, I tend to be more motivated to exercise. Both things increase my energy level, and increased energy is a great way to nurture creativity.

There are a lot of opinions out there when it comes to diet and exercise, and since this isn't my area of expertise, I won't go into specifics.

Regardless of which philosophy you follow, we can probably all agree that it's best to avoid processed foods, and it's best not to sit on our butts all day, even if we make a living doing something sedentary.

If you find it difficult to plan menus and grocery shop, a service such as Blue Apron may be a good option for adding more real food to your diet.

If you don't like to exercise, you can, at the very least, make a point of getting up and moving throughout the day, taking a daily walk, and doing some stretching exercises.

Blogger's Quick Guide to Blog Post Ideas. . • 38

Feed Your Spirit

THE TIMES IN MY LIFE WHEN I'M MOST CREATIVE often coincide with the times when I'm most alive spiritually. When I begin to neglect spiritual disciplines, I become more lethargic, and sometimes even a little depressed. At times, it's hard to break out of that slump, but it's worth making an effort to do so because it positively impacts every area of my life. When I'm right with God, I'm at peace and more creative, so it's hands-down the best way for me to feed my blogging soul.

Another benefit of feeding your spirit is that in addition to your alone time, there's often a community aspect such as belonging to a church. Since everyone, including introverts such as myself, benefit from relationships with others, plugging into a spiritual community is a great way to feed your blogging soul.

Blogger's Quick Guide to Blog Post Ideas. . • 40

Take Public Transportation

Depending on where you live, you may or may not have good public transportation options. But if you do, next time you need to go somewhere, instead of hopping in your car, take a bus or train.

I've discovered that when I take public transportation, I end up seeing the world in an entirely different way. I notice shops and other buildings I've never noticed before, pay more attention to people and what's going on around me, and take in the beauty of the world. I also sometimes meet interesting people and have fascinating conversations. Conversations I overhear sometimes spark thoughts and ideas. I can also daydream a bit, so long as I don't daydream so much I miss my stop!

All of these things are possible when I take public transportation. Since I don't have to focus on driving, my mind is freed up in a way that enhances creativity.

Blogger's Quick Guide to Blog Post Ideas. . • 42

Be a Life-Long Learner

THE MORE YOU FILL THE WELL of your mind with information, the more you have to draw on when it's time to come up with blog post ideas.

The interesting thing about this is that some of the things you learn that seem to be completely unrelated to your industry may end up being useful illustrations or stories in your blog. For example, let's say you read a true story about a man lost in the wilderness who, in spite of exhaustion, dehydration, and other physical challenges, kept going. You could use this story as an illustration in a blog post or book, even if you don't write about wilderness adventures.

The key thing to remember in this is that you can't continually put out more and more information without continuing to replenish your mind.

Regarding how to continually learn, my favorite ways are books, blogs, YouTube videos, and courses on sites such as Lynda.com and Skillshare.

Develop Your Own Blogging Rituals

THIS SECTION ON BLOGGING RITUALS is an excerpt from my book, *Blogger's Quick Guide to Writing Rituals and Routines*. While it's specific to writing rituals, the same things apply to coming up with blog post ideas.

What do you think of when you hear the phrase "blogging ritual"? Perhaps you think of some type of spiritual experience, with lit candles, burning incense, or Gregorian chants playing in the background. While all of those things can be part of a blogging ritual, your blogging ritual certainly doesn't need to include anything esoteric. In fact, even no-frills rituals can be effective.

Here's the deal: "ritual" is to some extent just another word for "routine." And while routines may not be exciting, they can be a key element in nurturing creativity.

Here are some benefits of blogging rituals:

1. They make it easier to get into your writing groove.

For instance, if you start every blog-writing session by brewing a certain type of tea, as soon as you begin to prepare the tea, your mind will transition into writing mode before you ever sit down at the computer.

2. They provide a sense of being in control.

When you participate in writing rituals, you are putting aside randomness and instability, and in a very real sense, taking control of your environment. Instead of allowing your day to control you, you are taking control of your day and strongly declaring that it is time to blog.

3. They reduce anxiety.

This point is built on the two previous points, because when you're able to quickly get into the writing groove and have a sense of being in control, you naturally feel less stressed.

4. They free your mind.

Mental clutter is one of the biggest hindrances to getting things done, and it most certainly impacts blogging productivity. When you establish blogging rituals, your mind shifts into a different mode, where the focus moves away from all of the other cares of life and business. This cleared mind helps you to write more freely, with fewer hindrances.

5. They expedite your entire writing process.

As I wrote earlier, blogging rituals make it easier to get into the writing groove. In addition to that, they tend to set off an entire process of routines that last beyond the actual ritual. For instance, not only will you start the writing process faster, with less procrastination, the sense of order present in the ritual will often spill over into the rest of the writing process.

When you consistently use the same routines, your entire writing process becomes more automatic. This order and automation reduces the amount of time you might waste with a more haphazard approach to your blogging

HOW TO COME UP WITH IDEAS

So now that you have a system set up for capturing ideas, and you are committed to doing things to nurture creativity, it's time to get some ideas down.

This section is the most extensive one in the book. If you implement them, you'll be well on your way to never running out of blog post ideas. But remember, this section builds on the other two, so don't skip setting up a system for capturing ideas, and don't think you can get away without nurturing creativity! All of the various parts fit together to complete the big picture of never running out of blog post ideas.

Blogger's Quick Guide to Blog Post Ideas. . • 48

Brainstorm

WHEN I FIRST STARTED OFF AS A BLOGGER, this was the only way that I came up with blog post ideas. It's easy and requires no special tools, and it works!

You can brainstorm by yourself or with a group. I personally find it far more effective and productive when I brainstorm alone, but do whatever works for you.

Here's something important to keep in mind. Not all of the ideas need to be good. In fact, the majority of them may be really bad. That's okay! Sometimes you have to come up with a lot of bad ideas to unearth some excellent ones.

The method I use is to simply set a timer and jot down ideas as fast and furious as I can. I like using the Pomodoro technique. The way that works is to set a timer for 25 minutes and write as many blog post ideas as you can before the timer goes off. Do not, I repeat, do NOT judge any ideas. If they pop into your head, write them down! When the timer goes off, take a five-minute break. After your break, set the timer for another 25 minutes and again, jot down ideas as quickly as you can. Speed is important because it keeps you from judging any of the ideas too harshly.

Remember, not all the ideas will be good. And that's okay! You can cherry pick ideas for the blog posts you'll actually write.

Blogger's Quick Guide to Blog Post Ideas. . • 50

Templates

IN MY FREE E-COURSE [5 Secrets to Developing the Blogging Habit](), one of the secrets that I share is to use templates. Now templates are great when it comes to helping you to write blog posts faster, but they can also help you come up with blog post ideas. Why? Because the templates are for different types of blog posts. For instance, you may have a template that deals with mistakes. Just looking at the template and considering that type of post can bring common mistakes that your target audience makes to mind.

Here's an article I wrote on how to use blog post templates: http://www.professionalcontentcreation.com/use-blog-post-templates-write-posts-less-time/

I also have some template packages available that start at $7, which you can get here:

http://www.professionalcontentcreation.com/templates/

Blogger's Quick Guide to Blog Post Ideas. . • 52

Speeches, Sermons, and YouTube Videos

IN THE PREVIOUS SECTION ON nurturing creativity, one of the things I mention is to be a life-long learner. You can do that by simply taking in information, for instance, by listening to podcasts when you're driving.

When it comes to actually getting some blog post ideas down, make a point of focusing more intently on the content you are taking in. One of the best ways to do that is to take copious notes. You can take notes in various ways. For instance, in addition to handwritten or typed notes, try sketchnoting, which is simply writing notes in a more visual form. And by the way, even if you don't feel you're artistic, give sketchnoting a try! It's one of my current creative endeavors, and it's helping me to retain information, even though my artistic skills are horrendous.

After taking notes, take a moment to read and reflect on them. Are there any illustrations you could use in a future blog post? If so, add them to OneNote, Evernote, or whatever system you've set up for capturing ideas. You can also make a practice of using this time to jot down at least five ideas for potential blog posts related in some way to the information you just consumed.

Blogger's Quick Guide to Blog Post Ideas. . • 54

Reading Notes

YOU CAN ALSO APPLY THE SAME methodology to reading as you do to listening to videos, sermons, and podcasts. Instead of being in a big hurry to finish a book, take the time to jot down some notes from each chapter. If the book you're reading is related to your industry, you can publish your reading notes as blog posts.

If you're not quite ready to publish your notes right away, add them, together with any ideas the book has sparked for your blog, to your blog post idea capturing system.

Blogger's Quick Guide to Blog Post Ideas. . • 56

Reviews

IN ADDITION TO TAKING NOTES on the books you read, you can also write book reviews. While a book review may touch on some of the key points in the book, they are different from reading notes in that they also offer a sort of critique. For example, you may include things that you agree or disagree with in the review, how the book compares to other similar books in the same genre, the quality of the research and writing, and whether or not you recommend the book.

You can also write reviews for products, services, events, and more.

In some cases, you can monetize reviews if you're an affiliate for the product. The important thing to remember, however, is to make sure to be honest in your review. Don't recommend a product just because you want to make a commission.

Here's an example of this type of post:

http://www.professionalcontentcreation.com/leadpages-vs-optimizepress/

To date, I've made $529.80 on this one article, as an OptimizePress affiliate. The key is that I really do use and love OptimizePress.

Now obviously, not all reviews have to be positive. It's important to share the truth about the products you review. My opinion is that unless you have a horribly negative experience with a product, it's not necessary to rake the creator of the product over the coals. Be honest but treat them the way you'd want them to treat you.

Blogger's Quick Guide to Blog Post Ideas. . • 58

Movie Reviews and Character Studies

IN THE SAME WAY THAT YOU CAN REVIEW books, you can also review movies. With both books and movies, you can draw and present lessons from the characters and how they apply to your niche.

Here's an exercise for you:

Set a timer for ten minutes and write down every single movie you can think of that you've seen in the past couple of years or beyond. Are there any lessons from the characters that could benefit your readers? What makes the characters in the movies heroes or villains? Jot down those ideas and add them to your primary idea capture system.

Heroes and Villains

Speaking of heroes and villains, here's a spin-off idea for you.

This is similar to the idea of using book or movie characters as inspiration, but you can draw inspiration from both real-life heroes and villains.

Here's an example of a fictional character and a real-life example:

- What Superman Can Teach You about _____
- Donald Trump's Biggest Failures and What Bloggers Can Learn from Them

Consider using current events for inspiration, but don't overdo it.

Blogger's Quick Guide to Blog Post Ideas. . • 60

Case Studies

CASE STUDIES ARE ONE OF THE MOST valuable types of content you can create for your readers because they take abstract ideas and make it clear how to apply them. For example, I could write a case study about how I used specific methods for coming up with blog post ideas.

In the case study, I could include the methods I used, the amount of time I spend working on the ideas, and the number of ideas I came up with in that amount of time. (Side note: I'm writing this down as an idea for a future blog post!) In the case study, I could also include any struggles that I had while using the technique, what worked and what didn't and how implementing the strategies impacted my overall site traffic.

The great thing about case studies is that they don't have to be just successes. If you don't mind being vulnerable, share where you failed, along with your success. Sometimes the best-case studies include a combination of both successes and failures. For instance, initially you may have failed at something and then changed your approach, and then had success. Including both aspects in your case study make the case study more valuable.

You can do case studies related to other people or businesses, as long as that information is available. Here's an example of how that would work.

Let's say that a topic you want to write on has to do with building a successful brand on YouTube. There is a lot of information about YouTube channels that is publicly available. For instance, you can see the number of subscribers that a channel has, how often they publish new videos, what they do to encourage people to subscribe, and how quickly their subscriber base grows. Pick the top ten channels and compare and contrast what the channels did and the results.

When you present case studies, give people takeaways that they can apply to their life or business.

Your Successes and Failures

THINK OF SHARING YOUR SUCCESSES and failures as a light version of a case study. Case studies often deal with hard facts and numbers. Successes and failures can involve a simple story that illustrates a point.

Here are some possible titles for this type of post:

- My Top 5 _____ (your industry or niche) Failures and What I Learned from Them about _____.

- My Worst Day as a _____.

- I Can't Believe How Much _____ (good or bad) Happened When I Did _____.

- This Surprisingly Easy _____ Made Me ____Dollars.

You get the idea!

When writing about your failures, start off by answering, "If I had it to do all over again, I would _____." For example, in my Blogger's Quick Guide Series, the third book I wrote was the *Blogger's Quick Guide to Starting Your First WordPress Blog*. Did you catch that it is the third book in the series? Do you think that perhaps that should have been the first book in a series on blogging? Me, too. The only problem is, I didn't think of it at the time. In fact, I didn't think at all about how the different books in the series might fit together or what they even would be before I started writing the first book. So, if I had it to do over again, I would have planned out the main topics for the series before writing the first book.

Writing about failures is pretty easy. I think most people like to read about people's failures more than their successes. Successes are good to write about as well, because people can learn from what you did right, and they also inspire people. But they can be a bit tricky, because it can seem like you're bragging. So, when you write about your successes, be sure to sprinkle in a healthy dose of humility as well, as no one likes someone who brags all the time.

Stories

COLLECT STORIES ON A REGULAR BASIS. You never know when a story may come in handy. Things that happen to you that are seemingly unrelated to your niche often make the best stories to use in your blog posts.

For example, as a young Army wife, I was pulled over on base for a random inspection. As part of the inspection, they went through the contents of my trunk. Later that day, I was horrified to discover that there were photos of naked, emaciated men in the trunk of my car. I always knew that one day I would use that story somewhere! I ended up using it in the post, "What I Learned about Blogging from the Naked Men in the Trunk of My Car," which you can read here:

http://www.professionalcontentcreation.com/learned-blogging-naked-men-trunk-car/

Here's another example. As a young woman, I overpacked for a trip to Europe. The heavy suitcases got the best of me at a train station. Here's how I used that story to illustrate what happens when you overload your life:

The luggage cart groaned beneath the weight of all my suitcases. I obviously loaded it with more than I should have. Nevertheless, I headed toward the long, steep, concrete ramp, as I attempted to steady the contents of the cart as I went.

As I made my way down the ramp, the cart gradually began to pick up speed until I could no longer control it. Pigeons, tourists, and cab drivers scrambled in a desperate attempt to get out of my way as I sped recklessly downhill.

By the time the wild ride was over, I had several cuts and bruises on my left shin. In spite of my injuries, I refused all offers of help, and with as much dignity as I could muster, held my head high and limped painfully to a waiting cab.

Although I've never been foolish enough to overload another luggage cart, I do have a tendency to overload my life. As I pile on extra obligations, the "luggage cart" of my life begins to speed out of control.

As usual, jot down the story in your blog post idea capture system. When you add the stories to your idea capture system, jot down some potential ways you can use the stories.

By the way, if you haven't done this in the past, think back to some funny, sad, or crazy things that have happened to you in the past and write them down in your idea capture system. You don't have to flesh out the stories or write them well at this point. Just jot down the facts so they'll be there when you need a good story to illustrate a point.

Spin-Off Posts

SOMETIMES THE BEST PLACE TO FIND blog post ideas is right underneath your nose – on your own blog. By using this exercise, you should be able to come up with at least ten blog post ideas. Here's how to write some spin-off posts based on your current blog post library:

1. Grab a piece of paper, a whiteboard, a notebook, or something else to write on.

2. Across the middle of the page, draw five circles.

3. In the circles, write the titles of the last five blog posts you've written.

4. Next, take one blog post title at a time, and see how many different spin-off blog posts you can write that are in some way related to the original post. For example:

   - Write a post based on a question left by one of your readers.

   - Take a post that is theoretical, and write an article that helps people implement the theory.

   - Write a post that presents the opposite point of view.

   - For every idea that you come up with, draw a line from the original circle to a square, and jot your idea in the square.

When you do this exercise, have an "anything goes" type of attitude. Remember, just because you jot an idea down doesn't mean that you need to use it!

Let's say that you do this exercise starting with five original blog posts (remember, you started by drawing five circles on your paper). Let's say that you come up with five potential spin-off blog posts ideas for each one. That would be 25 blog post ideas, and remember that the challenge that I'm presenting to you is to come up with only ten blog posts ideas. That means you can eliminate 15 of the ideas and still have plenty of ideas!

Digging Deeper

You may have enough ideas to keep you going for quite some time, but if you really want to come up with several weeks of ideas, then take this a step further, and do the same exercise again, with the spin-off blog post ideas you came up with in the above exercise.

Now obviously, the further you go with this, it's possible that the quality of the ideas will decrease, and you'll be very unlikely to want to use all of them, so pick and choose with care.

Tip for Newer Bloggers

This idea is geared more toward those who have enough blog posts already written. If you're a new blogger, you don't have that. . . yet. If that's the case, instead of doing this with your blog posts, use your blog post categories as your source of inspiration.

Holidays and Special Events

HOLIDAYS AND OTHER SPECIAL EVENTS provide a lot of inspiration for blog posts. When working on coming up with blog post ideas, be sure to consider the various holidays. Here are a couple of examples of the types of posts that holidays can inspire:

Martin Luther King Jr. Day – Blog posts about perseverance, peaceful resistance, how to be a history maker or someone people in your industry remember forever. For this particular holiday, you can also write about things more specific to the holiday such as prejudice and racial inequality, if those topics fit with the overall theme of your blog.

Christmas: Gift-giving guides, the greatest gift of all, winter recipes.

Halloween: The scariest moments in business.

Easter: How to resurrect a dying business, relationship, garden.

New Year's: Why every _____ deserves a fresh start, how to start the New Year off with a bang, how to set goals for the New Year.

For each of these, I simply thought of what the holiday represents, and then thought about how that could relate to blog posts.

Blogger's Quick Guide to Blog Post Ideas. . • 70

They Ask, You Answer

This is a method of coming up with blog post ideas that was made popular by Marcus Sheridan. In fact, he's written a book on the topic!

Marcus conducts workshops for business owners who need to come up with blog content. Among other things, he has everyone with the company write down ideas that customers and prospective customers have asked. They generally come up with more than ten ideas at a time.

Now you may not have a team, and that's fine. You can do this exercise by yourself as well. Simply jot down every single question that people have asked you related to your business. In the future, make this a habit. When people ask you a question, add it to your idea capture section.

Many times, people ask me a question via email. I use that as inspiration for my next blog post. I write and publish the post, and then send the person who emailed the question to me a link to the post.

Here's an example of a time I used a question sent via email as inspiration for a blog post:

http://www.professionalcontentcreation.com/ask-rebecca-know-readers-want-blog/

Blogger's Quick Guide to Blog Post Ideas. . • 72

Use Any Object

WHEN YOU LEARN TO LOOK FOR blog post ideas, you'll find ideas are everywhere. In fact, you can find blog post ideas in almost any object.

Here are some tips for finding blog post ideas using almost any object you see at any given time.

1. Pick an object, ANY object.

Don't think too long and hard about it — just select any object that pops into your head, or that you see in front of you. For the sake of example, the object I'll use is a car.

2. Jot down the parts of the object.

As an example, a car has tires, a steering wheel, brakes, mirrors, an engine, etc.

3. Make a quick list of uses for the object.

Again, using a car as an example, a car is used to transport people. It could be used to get you to work, to take a vacation, to visit a friend, etc.

4. Jot down problems associated with the object.

Car problems include things such as costing money, breaking down, potentially causing damage to objects and injury to people, etc.

---

5. Then list out all of the possible ways that what you've written above relates to your topic.

Whatever you do, in this step have an open mind, even if you think that the object you've chosen doesn't relate to your topic at all.

To prove it to you, I'll continue using a car as an example, and please note that as I wrote this, I had no idea where I was heading with it.

Car Parts and How They Relate to Blogging

Steering wheel

- What direction are you heading with your blog?
- How to know it's time to change the direction of your blog

Brakes

- What is slowing down the progress of your blog?
- Things you need to stop doing for your blog to succeed

Safety Belts

- 5 WordPress plugins to protect your blog
- How to keep your blog from being hacked
- How to avoid blogger burnout

Engine

- How to fuel blog post ideas

- How to give your blog a tune up

The Body of a Car

- Sleek blog design elements

- Blog themes that will turn heads

Horn

- Ways to get people to notice your blog without annoying the crap out of them

I could keep going and come up with numerous ideas using each of the starter ideas above, but I think that you most likely already have the idea and can apply this same thinking related to any object to your niche.

> *In fact, right now, it's your turn to do just that. Without thinking too long and hard about it, in your idea capture system, select an object that's unrelated to your industry and use it to inspire a list of blog post ideas.*

Blog a Book

IF YOU'VE EVER THOUGHT ABOUT writing a book but feel overwhelmed by it, or if you feel like you don't have time to write a book and blog, blogging a book is a way to kill two birds with one stone.

I won't say this is easy, because you essentially have to come up with an extensive outline for an entire book. But once you do, you'll have blog posts ideas to keep you going for a long time!

As an example, let's say you're going to write a 30,000-word book, and your blog posts are roughly 500 words each. That would be enough content for 60 blog posts. Since it's a good idea to make some of the content exclusive to the book, if you held back ten of those posts and then wrote a few extra things for the book, you'd have enough blog posts to last a year if you published one a week.

If you're interested in blogging a book, I recommend the book *How to Blog a Book* by Nina Amir.

Other People's Content

When I say to use other people's content for blog post ideas, I don't mean blatantly ripping off their content. However, you can read blog posts by your competitors and think about how you could write on similar topics but from a different perspective.

For example, you might have a completely different opinion and write a rebuttal to someone else's post. If you do this, be sure to link to the original post.

How to Spy on Your Competition

You can get a lot of great ideas for blog posts by spying on your competition. Before I get into the details of this idea, let me make it clear that spying is not the same thing as stealing. In other words, when you spy, you look at other blogs for inspiration, but don't simply rewrite what another blogger has published.

Now that I have that out of the way, here's how to go about getting blog post ideas by spying on your competition.

#1: Do a Google search for "top <your niche> blogs."

For example, if your industry is the dental industry, and you want to see how other dentists are using content marketing, you would type into Google, "Top dental blogs." (Be sure to remove the quotation marks when doing your search.)

#2: Look at several of the blogs, and bookmark any that look especially good.

What you're doing here is creating an "idea resource library." You can do the first two steps quickly, so there is no reason to delay doing them. Once you've bookmarked them, you can go back to them multiple times as you do your research.

#3: Check out the types of content they create.

Do they have written content? Podcast? Interviews? FAQs? Tutorials?

#4: What topics do they write about?

Jot down the main subject areas. One quick way to do this is to look at their blog categories. You can also quickly skim through their recent posts to get a feel for the topics they cover.

For example, in the blogging niche, I may see that some of my competitors write about how to make money blogging, affiliate marketing, WordPress tips, etc.

#5: Look for Popular Content

Make a note of any content that seems especially popular. For example, which content has a lot of comments and social media shares?

#6: Jot down ideas for how you could write on similar topics in a different way.

One key way to keep from ripping off other people's ideas is to make a couple of notes regarding ideas that come to you as you scan the blogs of your competitors. In other words, don't write detailed notes from someone else's blog post. Instead, simply make a note of the ideas someone else's content brings to mind.

Curate Other People's Content

Another way to use other people's content is to write curated articles. When you curate content, the best way to do it is to write a post where you link to the other content. You can write a summary of the other post, and then add your thoughts about the topic.

As a bonus, you can use this as an opportunity to reach out to someone else in your niche and let them know you linked to their article. Most bloggers appreciate this, and while you shouldn't expect anything in return, they may share the article with their readers. You never know how a relationship may develop from this approach.

Feedly

Subscribe to blogs in your niche using Feedly. Then regularly scan your Feedly feed for posts in your niche. Those posts can give you ideas for your blog, and you can also use some of the articles as references in your content.

I recommend sending articles that stand out to you in Feedly to either OneNote or Evernote for future inspiration and reference. I tell how to do this in OneNote in this article:

http://www.professionalcontentcreation.com/curate-content-using-onenote-and-feedly/

BuzzSumo

BuzzSumo.com is a great place to come up with ideas for blog posts. It's another way to use other people's content as a source of inspiration.

Essentially, the way that it works is to type in your keyword or a keyword phrase, and it will bring up the articles with the most social media shares for that topic.

This is another way to get inspiration from other people's content. What I recommend is looking at the articles and studying them. For example, what types of titles generate a lot of buzz? How long are the articles? What else about the articles may have caused the article to perform well? Can you improve on what they wrote? For instance, did they leave out some key points on the topic?

Also, scan any comments on the article as they may give you some ideas as well.

There is a paid version, but for free, you can do a limited number of searches.

Curate Your Own Content

IN THE SAME WAY THAT YOU CURATE other people's content, you can also curate your own. This works best once you have a good number of blog posts on similar topics. For example, once you have at least five to ten posts in a category, you can look at the possibility of curating it.

The key with this method is to find related posts and then link to them in a new post.

Use the title of the original posts as headings in the new post, and hyperlink to the original posts. Under each heading, write a summary of each post.

For this curated content, you can use titles such as:

- The Ultimate Guide to _____
- My Top Posts on _____

Blogger's Quick Guide to Blog Post Ideas. . • 84

Update and Repurpose Old Content

I DIVE DEEP INTO THE TOPIC OF content repurposing in my book *Content Repurposing Made Easy:*

http://www.professionalcontentcreation.com/CRME_book

I won't go into too much detail here, but here is the basic idea of how it works.

Take content that you've previously created and either add to it, update it, or put it into a different form. For example, you can take a blog post and use the content in it as material for a podcast. Or take a video that you created and create a written blog post using the information in the video.

Blogger's Quick Guide to Blog Post Ideas. . • 86

Interviews

INTERVIEWS ARE AN EXCELLENT WAY to have other people create content for you. Naturally, you need to prepare for the interview by coming up with good questions to ask. Sometimes that takes some research into the person or company.

The interview can be audio, video or written. Written form is the least demanding for you, since all you have to do is come up with the questions and then edit and upload the written answers returned to you.

For audio interviews, you can use a service such as Free Conference Call or Uberconference to record the call. Zoom is a popular option for recording video interviews.

Regardless of which type of interview format you use, be sure to make it worthwhile for the interviewee. For instance, give them an opportunity to give a plug for their new book or program or free giveaway.

Blogger's Quick Guide to Blog Post Ideas. . • 88

Get Guest Contributors

ONCE YOUR BLOG GROWS, other people may be interested in writing blog posts for you. If you go this direction, make sure the guest contributor is on the same page with you and will write content that fits with your audience. Guest blogger guidelines help.

Here's an example of guest contributor guidelines that you can adapt for your blog:

NameOfSite.com Editorial Guidelines

Thank you for your interest in writing for _____. Our standards are high because we strive to be the BEST source of content for _____. These guidelines are to help us accomplish that goal together. Thank you for partnering with us!

If you have any questions regarding anything in this document, please email _____.

Here are important things to keep in mind for every article you submit for inclusion on _____.

#1: First Rights

We require first rights to your article. First rights simply mean that your article shouldn't be published elsewhere, including your own website, before being published on _____.

You also grant us the right to keep the article on _____ for as long as we'd like.

You may publish the article on your own or other sites two weeks (or later) after it's been published on _____.

If any images were added to your post by the _____ team, please remove those images before publishing the article elsewhere.

#2: Our Audience

Our primary audience is _____.

Their primary job titles are _____.

#3: Primary Content Topics

Write a bit here about the types of topics you want to have covered. Think in terms of your broad categories, rather than specific titles.

The key thing to keep in mind with your content is that it needs to: _____.

Please do not closely duplicate content already published on _____. We want to offer up fresh content to our readers, rather than simply giving them a rehash of what we've already published.

#4: Article Length

Our articles are typically 800-2000 words long, but shorter or longer posts could work, depending on the subject, or if additional rich media such as videos and screenshots are added to the post. The minimum word count is 500 words.

#5: Formatting

Articles should have short paragraphs, and in most cases, short sentences. Keep in mind that most people skim articles online and are turned off by huge blocks of text.

Use subheads to break up the text and to increase the interest of the "skimmers."

#6: Links

Use links when appropriate

Bold the words you want hyperlinked, and then put the link information in brackets. For example:

XYZ point [LINK to xyz.com/abc]

Make sure the link(s) adds value to the piece.

You may link to a maximum of one of your own articles within the body of your article, or you may include a link to one of your videos on YouTube, Vimeo, etc.

Do not include affiliate links or links to anything that is primarily promotional such as a sales page. (You will have an opportunity to put something more promotional in your bio if desired.)

When appropriate, please link to at least one piece of content published on _____ or on the _____ YouTube channel.

#7: Images

When appropriate, include images such as screenshots with your article.

Images should not exceed 640 pixels wide.

If you include images with your post, please email them as an attachment, rather than pasting them in the body of your document.

In the body of your article, be sure it's clear where any images go, e.g., [ADD IMAGE name here].

#8: Bio

While your bio shouldn't feel overly salesy, you may include up to two links in your bio. Possible link options include a link to your website, social media profiles, an opt-in page, etc. Your bio should be 50 words or less.

#9: Headshot

Please include a professional-looking headshot in .jpg or .png format.

#10: Article Submission

When your article is complete, please email it attached as a Word document to _____.

#11: Right to Reject and/or Edit

We reserve the right to reject or edit any submission. If we do substantial editing, we'll run the article by you at least one week before publication.

#12: When Your Article Is Published

We'll notify you of the date that your article will go live.

Please share the article on your social media platforms and/or via email.

Please respond to comments for a minimum of one week after the post is published.

For your convenience, I've created an editable editorial guidelines template which you can get for free, here: http://www.professionalcontentcreation.com/editorial-guidelines-template/

Series Articles

SERIES ARTICLES ARE AN EXCELLENT WAY to create content that Google loves. The basic way it works is to keep adding to a previously published post and then republish it. Keep the same URL as the original article.

Each time you republish the article with new content, you can let your email subscribers and social media followers know that you updated the content.

This is a great way to end up with a blog post that's an ultimate guide to something in your industry. For example, let's say that the original article has 800 words. Add 800 more words to it a few weeks later and republish your article that is now 1600 words. When you add another 800 words to it, the article is then 2400 words and so on.

Depending on how far you want to take this, you could end up with 10,000 words or more on this one article. Not only will this be a great resource for your readers, assuming it's a quality article, it will also likely be shared a lot and rank well in Google and other searches.

Blogger's Quick Guide to Blog Post Ideas. . • 94

Trends

UNLESS YOU HAVE A SITE THAT NEEDS frequent updates, such as a celebrity gossip, sports, or news site, I generally recommend writing evergreen content. In case you're unfamiliar with the term, evergreen content is content that is still valuable in the days, weeks, months, and in some cases even years to come.

But there's something to be said for writing about trending topics. For example, in election season, blogging about any of the candidates may bring some new traffic your direction. The traffic may be short-lived, but if you write the post well and provide links to some of your other content, it may be a way for people to sign up for your email list, etc. You may just gain new fans. Just be sure that the way you spin the topic fits with the overall topic of your blog.

You can find trending topics on Facebook and Twitter and [Google Trends](.).

Blogger's Quick Guide to Blog Post Ideas. . • 96

Weekly or Monthly Themes

IF YOU'VE EVER BEEN RESPONSIBLE for planning and preparing your family's meals, you know how challenging it can be to come up with ideas week in and week out.

One of the best things I ever did that made this easier was to come up with themes for different nights of the week. For example, cooking Italian food on Monday, Mexican on Tuesday, and soups or stews (in the winter) or main-dish salads (in the summer) every Wednesday. I still had to plan, but just having those themes in place made my life easier. For example, I knew that on Tuesday we'd have either tacos, tamales, enchiladas, fajitas, or nachos.

Themes on your blog can also provide a framework that makes coming up with ideas easier. For instance, you may have a Motivational Monday video every Monday, a regular blog post on Wednesdays, and a case study every Friday.

Or if you blog just once a week, and you have four main categories on your blog, you could publish an article related to one category the first week, an article related to another category the second week, and so on.

Blogger's Quick Guide to Blog Post Ideas. . • 98

Ultimate List Posts

ULTIMATE LIST POSTS ARE OFTEN VERY popular and are shared a lot because they are a great resource for people. Here are some examples of titles for ultimate list posts:

- The Top 10 Honeymoon Destinations
- The Ultimate Guide to _____
- The Best 50 Resources for _____
- The Top 25 Books for _____

The point of these posts is that they help people find what they need on a particular topic. For example, if you were looking for a great place to go for your honeymoon, a blog post that had ten honeymoon destinations would help you out tremendously because someone already did a lot of the research for you.

As is always the case, in addition to just listing the items and linking to them, be sure to add at least a few sentences for each item explaining why it's the best or what your readers can gain from the specific resources or item you recommend.

Divide Posts

Have you ever noticed how conversations sometimes meander? You start off talking about one thing, and before you know it, you've talked about several other things as well.

This meandering also happens at times when we write. The thoughts may be good ones but perhaps a bit off from the original topic and intent of the post.

If you find this happening, instead of deleting the off-topic portion of a post draft, cut and paste it into a new document and use it as the basis for a new post. Chances are you already have a good start on a new article, so there's no reason to let that writing go to waste!

You can also divide posts that are getting too long. However, Google actually favors long-form content, so if all the points in your long article fit with the title and theme of the post, you may want to keep them in the original post. An exception to this is if you strive to keep your posts a certain length. For instance, if all of your posts are typically between 700 and 1000 words, and you have one that is turning out to be 3000 words and has three or four main points, you may want to divide it into three or four posts.

Use the Researcher Option in Microsoft Word

DEPENDING ON THE VERSION OF Microsoft Word that you have, you may or may not have this option. To see if you do, or how to get it if you don't, at the top of your Word document where it says, "Tell me what you want to do" type in "researcher." When you do so, it will bring up an area in the right sidebar where you can search for research materials. It includes citable sources, quotes, and even images – and it will even build a bibliography for you. So, you can use it not just for blog post ideas but for content to help you create the post.

As an example of how this helped me come up with an idea I never would have on my own, when I typed in the word "blogging" in this tool, one of the things that came up was an article on blogging in Iran. Among other things, it gave the history of blogging in Iran, and how when following a crackdown on Iranian media, blogging was a way that people could provide and find political news.

I could use this article not just to write about blogging in Iran, but how blogging gives people a voice.

You never know what you might find through this tool, but be sure to check it out to see if it's available in your version of Microsoft Word.

Comments on Blog Posts, YouTube Videos, and Facebook Groups

I MENTIONED GETTING INSPIRATION FOR blog posts from comments on articles you find on BuzzSumo. You can also do this in other places such as on YouTube videos, in forums and private Facebook groups related to your industry, and so on.

The comments that people leave, which often includes questions or frustrations, are a great way to discover ideas for content that will help your target audience.

One caveat is to not use the comment verbatim without permission.

Blogger's Quick Guide to Blog Post Ideas. . • 106

Experiences of Friends and Family

SOMETIMES IN CONVERSATIONS WITH friends and family members, you'll get ideas for blog post ideas.

There are a couple of things to be aware of here. The first is to respect the privacy and dignity of others. For example, if your child does something that would provide a great illustration in a blog post but could embarrass them if you share it, be sure to ask them for permission first.

As an alternative, you can use the basics of the real event, and then change some of the details, such as gender, name, and other identifying information, to protect the identity of the person that is the "star" of the story.

Amazon

AMAZON IS A TREASURE TROVE OF IDEAS for blog posts. For one thing, there is a ton of content on Amazon on every imaginable topic. Here are a couple of ways to use Amazon for blog post ideas.

First, check to see what books are selling best in your niche. You can find the link to the bestsellers here: https://www.amazon.com/gp/bestsellers/books

While books are different from blog posts, scanning through the bestsellers can give you a hint about which topics are doing well.

Next, read through the table of contents of books to see the types of things covered in the books. As always, you want to use this information not to copy but for inspiration.

Finally, the reviews also give some great insight into the types of things that people like about the book – or even better, what they don't. Sometimes the negative reviews give insight into what people really want to have covered in that niche.

For example, without planning this out ahead of time, I'm going to pick a topic outside of my niche and spend ten minutes getting blog post ideas from Amazon. I'm setting my timer now and will get back to you and share my results. Hang tight!

Ten Minutes Later. . .

I decided to look at the bestsellers in health, fitness, and dieting. In ten minutes, I came up with the following 25 ideas for blog posts titles.

#1: Is the Whole 30 Diet a Scam?
#2: Is the Whole 30 Diet Healthy?
#3: What is the Whole 30 Diet?
#4: What are Negative Calories?
#5: How to Develop Healthy Eating Habits
#6: Top Ten Green Smoothie Recipes
#7: European Secrets to Happy Living
#8: How to Have Joy in Any Circumstance
#9: Pregnancy Myths and Fairytales
#10: The Impact of Mindset on Health
#11: How to Have a Healthy Mindset
#12: How to Beat Your Sugar Addiction
#13: What Did Jesus Eat?
#14: How Going Gluten-Free Could Change Your Life
#15: The Three-Step Plan to Losing Belly Fat
#16: 52 Weeks of Low-Calorie Meals
#17: How to Eat Healthy in a Family of Junk Food Addicts
#18: How to Add Ten Years to Your Life
#19: How to Get a Good Night's Sleep
#20: Healthy Ways to Speed Up Your Metabolism
#21: The Top Essential Oils for Curing Insomnia
#22: The Top Ten Super Foods You Can Order Online
#23: The Top Ten Super Foods You Can Buy at Any Grocery Store
#24: Why People Who Eat Bacon Live Longer Than Vegetarians
#25: Why Dietary Supplements Are a Waste of Money

Note that I chose this topic on a whim, but even so, I was able to come up with some potential blog post ideas very quickly. As is always the case, after evaluating them, I would perhaps choose not to write some of them, but I'm sure several of them would work.

Blog Post Title Generators

I OFFER THIS NEXT SUGGESTION WITH a bit of trepidation because it has some real drawbacks. At the same time, when used correctly, it provides some excellent blog post ideas.

The way that blog post title generators work is that you plug in a topic related to your blog and the blog post title generator will, as the name implies, generate blog post titles.

Sounds easy, right? The good news is that it is easy. The bad news is that sometimes the titles generated are, well, amusing at best and horrible at worst.

For example, when I typed "blog post titles" into it, the first suggestion was, *Why Blog Post Titles are Scarier than Tyra Banks.* Hmmm. . . Somehow, I don't think that's quite right.

Let's try another one: *Why Mom Was Right about Blog Post Titles.* This one has possibilities since it would stir up curiosity. This is, of course, assuming that things my mom (or a "typical" mom) says could apply to blog post titles.

Here's another one: *How Blog Post Titles Changed How We Think about Death.* Wow. This one is even worse than the Tyra Banks one.

Let's try just one more: *What Experts Are Saying about Blog Post Titles.* Okay, this is the best one yet.

So, here's the deal. I shared these computer-generated titles with you to make a point. Nothing replaces the human mind. When it comes right down to it, this little title generator doesn't understand my topic or my audience. What it does, however, is spark some ideas to which I can add a human touch.

If you decide to use a blog post title generator, here are a few for you to try:

Portent's Content Idea Generator:

https://www.portent.com/tools/title-maker

HubSpot's Blog Topic Generator:

http://www.hubspot.com/blog-topic-generator

BlogAbout Blog Title Generator:

https://www.impactbnd.com/blog-title-generator/

Jargon

MOST INDUSTRIES HAVE industry-specific jargon. Make a list of the jargon in your industry. You can then write a "glossary" post that explains all the jargon, or you can devote individual blog posts for each term.

For example, in the blogging industry, CTA, which means "call to action," is a common acronym. I could write a blog post about how to write a compelling call to action.

Blogger's Quick Guide to Blog Post Ideas. . • 114

Keyword Tools

KEYWORD TOOLS SUCH AS BING OR GOOGLE are great ways to find blog post ideas. The basic way they work is to type in a keyword related to your industry and see what comes up. As is always the case, not all the ideas are worth using, but many of them are.

One wonderful thing about using keyword tools is that you can see how many people search for those keywords, which can help you evaluate whether or not they are worth using. Here's where you can find the keyword tools:

Google: www.google.com/AdWords/KeywordTool

Bing: www.bing.com/toolbox/keywords

Blogger's Quick Guide to Blog Post Ideas. . • 116

Be Negative

I'M A SUPER POSITIVE PERSON, so it kind of rubs me the wrong way to suggest that you use negativity to come up with blog post ideas.

But here's the deal: Regardless of your industry, there is some negativity. For example, if you have a natural health blog, you know some people think natural health is a sham. Instead of being defensive about it, address the criticisms head on. Write about the concerns and what to do about them. Do your best to present the information in a balanced manner, and you just may win over some of the naysayers.

Here's another example: Let's say you own an appliance company, and one of your products is glass-topped stoves. You can write an article about the five top problems with glass-topped stoves. You can then, of course, include information on what to do about the problems.

One reason why these types of posts are so effective is that people look for negative information on something before making a commitment. For instance, if I was thinking about buying a glass-topped stove, I would research and try to find reasons not to buy one first. If your article addressed that issue, and yet assured me that the problems were not ones to be overly concerned with, or that the advantages outweighed the disadvantages, that would encourage me to buy one – hopefully from you.

So, the bottom line is, don't shy away from writing about the negative aspects of your product or industry. This honesty will help to make you a trusted source that people will go to again and again.

Select Your Blog Post Idea Methods

I've given you several different ways to come up with blog post ideas. I recommend starting with three to five that resonate the most with you. You can also jot down a list of other methods you'd like to try in the future, so that any time you're stuck, you'll be able to quickly generate ideas.

Evaluating and Using Ideas

By this point, if you've followed the recommendations in this book, you should have an endless supply of blog post ideas or at the very least, know how to come up with ideas any time you need them.

I recommend doing idea generation on a regular basis. But coming up with ideas is only the first part. You need to then evaluate your ideas and determine which ones to use. I then recommend adding your ideas to an editorial calendar of some type. Your editorial calendar can be anything from a Google or Outlook calendar to a spreadsheet or a WordPress plugin such as CoSchedule.

Your last step is to write the blog posts. To make the most out of your blog posts, I recommend my blog post checklist. This checklist is generally only available as a component of my blog post template packages, which you can get here: http://www.professionalcontentcreation.com/templates/

However, as a special thank you to those who have purchased this book, I've made the blog post checklist available individually for $7 here:

http://professionalcontentcreation.com/blog_post_checklist

Conclusion

I HOPE THAT YOU FOUND THIS BOOK on how to come up with blog post ideas helpful.

As a brief refresher, here are the key points, and assignment for you.

#1: Analog or Digital

Determine where you want to use an analog or digital system (or a combination of the two) for capturing blog post ideas.

#2: Set Up Your Blog Post Idea Capture System

Decide one which one, or two systems you want to use and set things up. For instance, if your two systems are OneNote and 3x5 cards, create a OneNote notebook for capturing ideas, and purchase some 3x5 cards, along with accessories such as binder clips or rings.

#3: Add "Soul-Nurturing" Activities to Your Calendar

Review the section on nurturing creativity and determine what changes you need to make in your life and routine to nurture your blogging soul. For instance, you may decide that you need to improve your sleep habits and go on a weekly artist date. Jot down any ideas you want to implement, and when appropriate, schedule activities such as artist dates on your calendar.

#4: Come Up With 100 Blog Post Ideas

Review the How to Come Up with Ideas section and implement one to five of the suggestions. Make it your goal to come up with at least 100 ideas.

So that you never run out of ideas, add "generate blog post ideas" to your calendar on monthly or quarterly basis.

Other Books by Rebecca Livermore

To check out my entire selection of books, visit my Amazon Author Page at amazon.com/author/rebeccalivermore.

Courses by Rebecca Livermore

If you enjoy video content, along with an opportunity to connect with me personally and other students, check out my courses on Skillshare: https://www.skillshare.com/r/user/rlivermore.

At the time of this writing, using the link above, you can join Skillshare for 99 cents for the first month, and only $8-12 per month thereafter. It's my favorite online learning hub, and there are thousands upon thousands of amazing courses there, all included in the subscription price.

I plan to add multiple courses on blogging, writing, business, and personal development and hope to see you here: https://www.skillshare.com/r/user/rlivermore

About the Author

Rebecca Livermore is a bestselling author, blogger, and the owner of Professional Content Creation, a company focused on helping business owners use content to market their businesses. She has worked as a freelance writer since 1993 and has served as a content manager for top bloggers such as Michael Hyatt, Amy Porterfield, and Marcus Sheridan. Her passion is helping others integrate faith and business in their blogs, books and all other aspects of content creation.

She has been married to her husband, Chuck, for more than 30 years and is the mother of two young adults who affectionately nicknamed her, "Hot Rod Mama."

www.ingramcontent.com/pod-product-compliance
Lightning Source LLC
Chambersburg PA
CBHW020919180526
45163CB00007B/2801